KU-614-352

fast
thinking:
your own
interview

(▶) **say the right things**

(▶) **be impressive**

(▶) **get that job**

SANDWELL LIBRARY & INFORMATION SERVICE	
I1779073	
Cypher	03.01.03
650.14	£5.99

contents

introduction

It's that vital job interview tomorrow, the one that could transform your career, and you still haven't begun to prepare for it. You've no idea what you're going to wear, what you're going to say, or how you're going to answer all those nightmare questions you know they're going to ask. You're probably wondering how you could have left it this late, but it's happened now. Life's too fast, work's too full, and somehow this is your first chance to think about winning that job.

It may be little consolation, but you're not the only one. Your job interview may be crucial to you, but it's hardly going to be at the top of your boss's priority list, so it frequently gets pushed to the back of the queue. But don't panic. Plenty of people don't start preparing for job interviews until the night before – or even later – and the ones who think smart and act fast still manage to clinch the job. It's not too late for you to be one of them.

This book will show you how. Sure, most books tell you to put aside loads of time to prepare thoroughly, and if you have loads of time you can certainly put it to good use. But the type of people who succeed at high-flying or ambitious job interviews aren't generally the kind who have a lot of spare time, are you? So let's get real. A few hours is all you have at most, and you want:

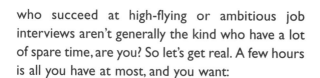

- **tips** for making sure you come across as a winner
- **shortcuts** for looking good without hours of preparation
- **checklists** to make sure you're ready for all those tricky questions

... all put together clearly and simply. And short enough to read fast, of course.

You may be reading this and thinking, 'A few hours to prepare? I should be so lucky!' I know, it does occasionally happen that you don't start preparing until you're on your way to the interview. I'm not condoning it, but then I'm sure it wasn't your ideal choice either. It makes winning the job tougher, but it can still be done. And just for you, there's a section at the back of this book on preparing for your interview in 15 minutes. You can't say fairer than that.

So if you were thinking of panicking, forget it. Save it for something more deserving. This one little volume contains all you need to know to give your best interview ever, even if it's only a couple of hours away. If you have longer than that to prepare, you've no business complaining about the timescale. It's going to be a breeze. You've even got time to make yourself a cup of coffee before you start.

work at the speed of life

This book will guide you, chapter by chapter, through the critical stages of preparing for a successful interview:

1. The first thing you need to do is establish your objective. If you're not clear exactly what you're trying to achieve, you will seriously reduce your chances of achieving it.

2. You need to be prepared for the interview, however little time you have. So we'll see how to make the best use of your limited time.

3. The attitude you convey during your interview will have a big impact on how well you impress the interviewers, so we'll have a look at what you need to do to give the best first impression you can and follow it through for the rest of the interview. Yes, even if it's an internal job you're applying for.

4. Now we're down to the nitty gritty. The more prepared you are for how the interview will proceed, the better

you will handle it. Chapter 4 will tell you what format to expect, and what the interviewers will want to know.

5. Sooner or later, they start asking you questions. And how will you answer them? Chapter 5 will give you checklists of the most likely questions and how to answer them, and – before you're tempted to panic again – the toughest questions and how to respond effectively.

6. Just before they get to the end, they always ask you, 'Have you got any questions?' And you feel like a pillock sitting there blankly saying, 'Duh ... I don't think so.' Well, this time, you'll have questions. Intelligent ones. Trust me.

7. Most people dread being given tests at an interview. Even if you think the tests themselves are fun, you don't want your career to hang on the results. So we've included a brief guide to handling psychometric and other tests.

8. Some of us are deeply affected by nerves at interviews. It's hardly surprising – the outcome of a job interview can change your life. But it's hardly helpful either. So if you're one of those people who feels that your performance at interview is affected detrimentally by nerves, you'll find some useful tips in Chapter 8.

9. And what happens after the interview? It's important to follow up the interview effectively whether or not you get the job, and whether the job is internal or external. So you'll find the guidelines for making the most mileage out of your interview in this Chapter 9.

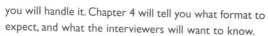

This one little volume contains all you need to know to give your best interview ever, even if it's only a couple of hours away

fast thinking gambles

If it's so easy to prepare for an interview in a couple of hours, why do all the books tell you to give yourself longer? Why not simply schedule an hour or so before you leave for the interview to get yourself in the frame? Well, the fact is that you will maximise your chances if you give yourself longer. A couple of hours will give you time to come across well, and if you're the best candidate it will show and you'll get the job.

But what if the competition is tight? When that happens, little things can make a difference. And the extra time might have enabled you to score a few extra brownie points. Otherwise, there's always an element of risk.

- You might not have anticipated a tricky question which you would have thought of if you'd given yourself longer to prepare.

- Ideally, you should thoroughly research the organisation you're applying to work for. If you leave all your preparation to the last minute, your lack of research may show. It won't affect your ability to do the job, but it won't reflect well on you.

 During the course of preparation, you may realise that you could really impress your interviewer if you took along a copy of that brilliant report you wrote last summer, or the letter of congratulation from your MP after you organised that corporate charity event that raised £10,000 for the local hospital. But it's too late to get hold of them now ... if only you'd started thinking about the interview sooner.

The preparation doesn't need to take more than a few hours at the most, but ideally it should start a few days ahead, as you can see. That gives you time to get hold of your prospective employer's annual report, dig out the best material from your own portfolio, think through all the questions you need to prepare for, even rehearse the interview with friends or colleagues.

Fast thinking and smart action will get you through the interview this time, and with a modicum of luck none of the small holes that are left in your preparation will show. In any case, there won't be any large holes. But if you want a copper-bottomed guarantee that you've covered everything you could possibly need to, you'd better start a couple of days earlier another time.

Fast thinking and smart action will get you through the interview this time, and with a modicum of luck none of the small holes that are left in your preparation will show

1 your objective

Boring! 'Setting objectives': typical business-speak, isn't it? Well, no actually. That is to say, you may not like the terminology, but the action itself is vital (unlike a lot of genuinely boring business-speak). As with any journey, if you don't know where you're going, you may never arrive. In other words, if you don't know what you're aiming to achieve, you may not get the job. You need a clear focus to get you there, fast and effectively.

thinkingsfast

NO SECOND CHANCES

When you're trying to prepare for something fast, it's even more important than usual to set a clear objective before you begin. You haven't time to faff about trying different approaches and learning from your mistakes. You have to get it right first time. So investing a little time now in setting your objective will save you oodles of time later on.

Right, so we're agreed that we need to set an objective. So what is it? Surely the objective is to get the job? Indeed it is, but an objective that indicates *how* you're going to get the job is far more useful than one which doesn't. Your specific aim is *to get the job by demonstrating to your prospective employer that you are the best person for it.*

But we can do better than that. We can be more specific so that the objective is more useful. And we can do that by specifying *in what way* you will be the best person for the job. So try this for an objective: *to get the job by demonstrating to my*

TAILORED OBJECTIVE

Sometimes, for example with internal posts, you happen to know that your interviewer is giving priority to a particular aspect of the candidates' record. Maybe they are very keen to find someone with experience of dealing with tough complaints, or someone who can already use certain equipment. You can build this kind of information into your objective. For example: *to get the job by demonstrating that I am the best person for the post of customer services manager in terms of experience, ability, personality and, in particular, handling difficult complaints.*

prospective employer that I am the best person in terms of experience, ability and personality.

That's more like it. That's more helpful than simply stating your objective as 'to get the job'. Now you know exactly where to focus your energies.

SO WHAT?

So what are you going to do with your objective, now you've got one? How is it going to help? Well, a good objective is a touchstone against which you can measure everything you do. If you're pushed for time, and you can't do everything, your objective will tell you which things to do: those things that help you meet it.

So, for example, if you haven't time to research your prospective employer thoroughly *and* call in at the office on your way to the interview to pick up a copy of your acclaimed report, your objective will help you decide which to do. Your brilliant report might do more to persuade your interviewer that you really are qualified to do the job than the fact that you know their last year's accounts by heart. So call in and collect it on your way (making a mental note for next time that if you'd left yourself longer, you could have done both).

See? Your objective helps to keep you focused on what's really important, and when you're under time pressure, that's crucial. Now you have your objective clear, write it down so you can have it in front of you all the time as a reminder to keep you on the straight and narrow.

for next time

Set your objective as early as possible. It won't vary a great deal from job to job, but the sooner you have it fixed in your mind, the more focused – and therefore quicker – all your preparation will be.

2 be prepared

You're a salesperson. It doesn't matter what the job you're applying for is – from accountant to despatch manager – you are a salesperson at your interview. Your purpose is to sell yourself to the interviewer as the best candidate for the job. And any good salesperson prepares thoroughly to make a big, important sale like this one.

Ok, so you're not exactly wallowing in spare time here. But you can still find time for some vital work on making yourself as saleable as possible. Simply reading this book is a big part of your preparation. But if you have time for it, even more work will stand you in even better stead. In particular, you need to:

- ▶ **Research your prospective employer.**
- ▶ **Prepare your own case.**
- ▶ **Be ready for the interview itself.**

RESEARCH YOUR PROSPECTIVE EMPLOYER

Your interviewer will expect you to have done your homework and found out what you can about them. But this isn't meant to be some kind of psychological obstacle course; they're not trying to make it difficult for you. So there's no need to make sly, underhand approaches to various parts of the organisation pretending to be a customer or a prospective shareholder. Simply phone your contact at the organisation and say, 'Could you send me some information about the company, please?' And while you're there, ask for a copy of the job description for the post you're applying for if they haven't sent you one automatically.

If they dither, or don't get round to sending you the information, call the sales department and ask for a copy of their brochure. There's no need to say why you want it but, if they ask, be honest. You've got an interview and you'd like to know more about the company and its products. If you've left it too late to get anything through the post, turn up early for the interview and spend 15 or 20 minutes looking through any company material you can find in reception.

ONLINE RESCUE

If you've left it too late to get anything sent in the post, you may well be able to get all the information you need on the Internet. If you have access, and the company has a website, you're in business.

You're going to use all this information you research for two purposes. First, you're going to show that you had the initiative and enthusiasm to research the company (yes, *you* know you didn't start until you arrived at reception half an hour ago, but *they* don't). In order to do this, you'll have to make sure the interviewer discovers your intimate knowledge of their organisation. So make sure you drop it into the conversation as you go along: 'I like the idea of working for a growing company, and I notice your profits have increased by at least 5 per cent a year for the last four years.' That sort of thing.

If you only have time to absorb two or three facts about the organisation, make sure they're pertinent ones and then make sure you mention them. Your interviewer will assume you've done a great deal more homework than you really have.

The second use you will have for this information is to look for ways to demonstrate that you are the best person for the job. For example, you might say:

- 'I notice that you do a lot of business in France; I used to live in Paris so my French is fluent and I know their style of doing business.'

- 'Your delivery team seems to cover a wide geographical area. That can make managing the team tougher, can't it? I had exactly the same challenge to overcome in my last job.'

- 'I was very interested to see that you have a fully integrated website. I'm a great believer in the importance of the Internet right across organisations. I'm keen to work for an organisation that can help me learn more about how integration can work in every department.'

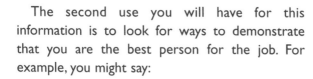

thinking smart

TRAVEL WISELY

If you have the option, travel to the interview by public transport rather than by car (leaving plenty of time for delays, of course). You can mug up on company information – and anything else – much more easily on a bus or a train than you can when you're keeping your eyes on the road.

If you only have time to absorb two or three facts about the organisation, make sure they're pertinent ones and then make sure you mention them

So, the more research you can find time for, the better. But even if you have time for very little, you can still make every bit of information you do manage to glean work for you.

PREPARE YOUR OWN CASE

The next part of selling yourself involves preparing your best selling points and being ready to present them effectively. You've got at least some information about the job you're being interviewed for; you may have plenty of information. So go through it and list the strongest points in your favour – the ones you really want to drive home. For example:

- relevant experience
- relevant qualifications
- relevant skills
- personality traits – good with people, perhaps, or a stickler for detail.

Make sure you know what you most want to say at the interview. Don't get home after it and think, 'Oh, dammit. I never mentioned that I used to organise all the delivery rotas when I worked at X&Co.' You should have thought of all these things in advance and be ready to say them the second an opportunity presents itself. Even when time is short, you can think through your key selling points. With more time, you can go into more detail.

Think about whether you have anything to show your interviewer that might impress on them how well suited you are to the job. This might include a portfolio of past work, press cuttings you have generated, reports you've written, certificates or proof of qualifications, testimonials and so on. Take anything portable which will help to sell you, and find a chance to show it to your interviewer.

BE READY FOR THE INTERVIEW ITSELF

No matter how late you've left your preparation, there are certain basics you really must remember.

thinking smart

KEEP THE MASTER

If you want to show your interviewer any examples of your work, or any certificates or testimonials, they may decide to hang on to them to look at later or show to colleagues. So make sure you give them copies rather than originals. If this is impossible, affix your name and address to the items so they can be returned to you.

The interview itself needs to go smoothly if you're going to win this job. So:

- Leave plenty of time to get to the interview.
- Take along the letter inviting you to interview giving the time, directions and so on.
- Take a phonecard or money in case you get lost and need to call for directions.
- Have a briefcase containing brochures about the organisation and your own portfolio material.
- Take a notepad and a pen.

When it comes to selling yourself ... well, you wouldn't give a presentation without knowing how long it was expected to last, would you? And the same goes for an interview. As it progresses, you have certain selling points to make – certain things you wish to say. Will you have time to say them all?

You need to know how long the interview is going to go on for. So ask. Phone your contact at the organisation and say, 'I wonder if you can tell me how much time has been allocated to my interview?' It's a perfectly reasonable question, and they should be happy to answer it. (You should ideally ask this at the same time you phone to ask for information about the organisation and a copy of the job description.)

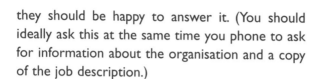

for next time

The sooner you start your preparation, the more chance you have of assembling all the information you need. In particular you want to collect:

▸ information about your prospective employer, including sales material, annual report, press cuttings, and so on
▸ the job description for the post you're applying for
▸ any material of your own, from examples of your work to testimonials, which will help to sell you as the best person for the job.

Some of this material can take time to track down or get hold of. Just a couple of 15-minute slots a week or two before your interview should be enough to get hold of most (or all) of what you need. If you leave it all until the last minute it may be too late.

You need to know how long the interview is going to go on for. So ask

3 your attitude

The way you come across as a person is going to have a big impact on how your interviewer assesses your suitability for the job. There's no need to pretend to be someone you're not, but you do need to come across as the most friendly, positive version of yourself. From first impressions to lasting impressions, you're more likely to get the job if your interviewer warms to you than if they don't.

FIRST IMPRESSIONS

It used to be easy to know how to dress for an interview. A smart suit and tie, or a well-cut skirt and blouse in muted colours, and Bob was your uncle. But these days it's not quite so simple. There are companies around now where everyone wears jeans and T-shirts to work, and turning up to an interview in a suit and tie will make you look as if you're simply not going to fit in.

So you need some kind of idea what the dress code for regular employees is. You may well have a pretty good hunch, of course, from the type of company it is. Media people usually dress casual, advertising people are often trendy, solicitors' offices tend to be formal, and so on. If you're applying for a new job in your own industry, you'll have a fairly clear idea already. If you're really stumped, though, the solution is the same as usual: just ask. Phone your contact, who may be your interviewer's assistant or secretary, and ask what the dress code is in the company. They won't mind – they'll be impressed you bothered to ask.

Having established what the organisation's style of dress is, however, don't wear it yourself unless

thinking smart

NEARLY NEW

Contrary to what you might think, an interview is no place to wear brand new clothes. This is not the time to be distracted by trousers that turn out to be painfully tight when you sit down, or a pair of shoes that have given you blisters before you even arrive, or a dress with straps that keep slipping. You want clothes that are new enough to look clean and smart, but which have at least been broken in.

it's pretty formal. You want to look as though you fit in, but also as though you've made a bit of an effort. So aim to dress a notch or two smarter than the regular employees. For example, if they all wear jeans and a T-shirt, wear chinos and an informal shirt, or a casual dress. You want to look like they would if they made an effort. The only exception is if they wear formal business suits. In this case you don't have to go for evening dress; just wear a formal business suit yourself.

The opening gambit

We all know about the importance of first impressions. The moment you meet your interviewer, greet them confidently and with warmth. Smile, step towards them, hold out your hand to shake and as soon as they introduce themselves say, 'Pleased to meet you,' or 'How do you do?' or whatever phrase you feel comfortable with. If there is more than one interviewer, shake each hand in turn. Wait to be invited before you sit down.

PROJECTING A POSITIVE IMAGE

Well done. You're in there and you've made a good, solid first impression. Now you simply need to keep up the good work. You need to make sure you continue to come across as the kind of person anyone would be proud to have working for them. As well as being polite and friendly, you need to be:

- ▶ *responsive*. Make an effort to give full answers to the questions your interviewer asks you, and volunteer relevant information. If they say, 'I see you trained as a zoo keeper originally,' don't just say, 'Yes.' Be more responsive: 'Yes, I love animals. But I found them so easy to get along with it wasn't challenging enough, which is why I decided to make the move into customer relations instead.' Never settle for one-word answers – they come across as sullen and unhelpful.

- ▶ *confident*. You may be feeling anything but confident, but confidence is an attractive quality in an employee so you need to show you have it. That doesn't mean being pushy or arrogant, though. It just means don't apologise for yourself. If your interviewer says, 'So, it's two years since you did any actual face-to-face selling,' don't say, 'I'm afraid so.' Say something like, 'It is, but I always feel it's one of those skills that you never lose once you've learnt it.'

- ▶ *energetic*. People who project life and energy come across as so much more enthusiastic and capable than those who seem flat and sluggish. So stay upbeat, sit up straight, speak clearly and make eye contact (with all your interviewers if there is more than one). Smile readily, and sound interested in what both you and the interviewer are saying.

NO SMOKING

It never helps your image to smoke in an interview, and it often harms it. Even if your interviewer is a smoker and offers you a cigarette, decline it. Smoking can give you an air of being too informal, laid back and relaxed – good qualities in general, but you should appear more keen to make a good impression at an interview that is important to you. Alternatively, a cigarette may make you appear nervous and neurotic; again, not the way you want to come across.

None of this requires you to put on an act, and none of it should distract you from answering questions and giving information that will help to sell you. It's just a matter of putting forward the most positive aspects of your personality.

Body language

It's worth mentioning body language, too. If you lean slightly forward in your chair you will look interested (if you really *are* interested, you will probably find yourself leaning forward slightly anyway). It's important to make frequent eye contact with your interviewer – all of them if you have more than one – so that they feel included, and so that you can gauge their response to what you're saying. Eye contact will enable you to pick up subtle signs of confusion, scepticism or, ideally, agreement in your listeners.

The last thing you want is to get so hung up on body language you get uncomfortable and can't concentrate on the conversation, so just avoid the extremes:

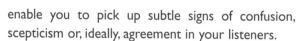

- Don't perch on the edge of your chair. Sit well back in it (unless it is a very deep upholstered easy chair, in which case there's a danger of looking too relaxed if you get lost right at the back of it!).

- Don't cover your face with your hands.

- Don't give off defensive signals by crossing your arms and your legs, and generally clutching yourself so you can't use your hands.

for next time

The best way to give a good impression at your interview is through practice. Get a reliable friend or colleague – one who is prepared to be honest – to play the part of the interviewer. Role-play the interview starting with the initial greeting, and then get them to invite you to sit down, and to ask you questions.

Practice with a few different chairs, have them greet you at the door or from behind a desk, and generally rehearse various options so you're prepared for anything by the time you get to the interview proper.

The last thing you want is to get so hung up on body language you get uncomfortable and can't concentrate on the conversation

4 what to expect

All interviews are pretty much the same, really. They might not feel like it from your end, but they all follow the same basic format in order to achieve the same result: to enable the interviewer to select the best candidate to fill the post. If you know what the interviewer is trying to do, and how they're trying to do it, it makes it easier for you. For one thing, it's easier to be confident when you know what to expect. And for another thing, you can impress the interviewer by helping the process along. So here's a quick guide to how the interview is likely to go.

THE INTERVIEWER'S JOB

As far as your interviewer is concerned, they have already sifted through probably dozens of application forms to narrow down the applicants to the few they are interviewing. You should take heart from this, because you must have something they like the sound of to get this far.

Their problem now is to interview the remaining candidates in order to decide which one to offer the job to. All the candidates will be very different, and have different strong and weak points, which is going to make it difficult. Should they opt for the candidate with the longest experience, or the one with the briefer but more relevant experience? Should they choose someone with a solid, reliable-looking profile, or someone who seems less stable but more creative and original? Should they plump for someone who will clearly fit in well with the team, or someone more reserved but with exactly the right qualifications?

It's a tough job being an interviewer, not that you'll be overflowing with pity for them. But they do have a handful of tools to help them make their choice. First of all, they should have a clear picture of the job they're trying to fill. They will know this from:

- ▶ **the job description, which gives them the overall objective of the job and outlines the key responsibilities**

- ▶ **the employee specification, which tells them the skills and attributes the successful candidate will need.**

And they already have a picture of each candidate from:

- your application form
- your CV.

They are trying to find the candidate who most closely matches up with the job on offer. So they're interviewing you to see if you're the one. Any half-decent interviewer will have two lists of questions: questions they are asking everyone, and questions specifically for you which they have formulated by looking through your CV and application form.

The interviewer probably won't have sent you a copy of the employee specification (that's a bit like showing someone the exam questions before they sit the exam). But at least you have everything else the interviewer has: the job description, your CV and your application form.

THE FORMAT

The interviewer will almost certainly follow this format:

- They will welcome you, and chat for a minute or two to put you at your ease.

thinking smart

I CAN DO THAT!

Go through the job description and work out the best way of demonstrating that you fit it well. Think what experience you have had that shows you can fulfil each of the key responsibilities. It may be editing a newsletter at school, organising volunteers at a charity you work for, or getting an Open University degree. Don't limit yourself to work experience only. Be ready to help the interviewer by showing you can do everything they need the successful candidate to do.

▶ They will ask you their general list of questions that everyone is being asked, for example, 'Tell me about your experience of dealing with customers face to face,' or 'What do you think are the most important qualities of a good manager?'

▶ Then they will ask you the specific questions that have arisen from your application form or CV, such as, 'I see there is a blank six months on your CV in the first half of 1999. What were you up to then?' or 'I notice you work at home two days a week at the moment. How do you find that fits in with managing a team?'

▶ When they have finished all their questions, they will fill you in on a few more specific details about the job and then ask you for your questions.

Go through the job description and work out the best way of demonstrating that you fit it well. Think what experience you have had that shows you can fulfil each of the key responsibilities

The interviewer is aiming for you to do most of the talking except right at the end when they tell you more about the job, from the size of the department to the standard working hours. So co-operate with them and give full and helpful answers to their questions.

ANY WORRIES?

If your interviewer has any concerns about your application they will want to explore them. They don't want to turn you down because they're suspicious of your six-month employment break, for example, when it might have been due to illness or maternity leave. Or maybe they're concerned that you haven't been promoted in five years at the same company, not realising that your job has increased in scope and responsibility along with your salary, but the job title has stayed the same.

If your interviewer has any such worries, they will ask about them. And – if they're worth their salt – they'll keep on asking until they get a satisfactory answer. You can help by being ready to recognise these kinds of questions and giving full answers to them. A good interviewer will probe until they feel they've got the answer they need, and if necessary they'll tell you their concerns. But in case they don't, you need to be ready to reassure them if you suspect they are worried.

The kind of things that worry employers are, for example:

- lack of specific relevant experience
- lack of relevant personal qualities; for example, the ability to handle people diplomatically, or a thorough approach to detailed work
- gaps in employment
- failure to progress up the career ladder as fast as they would expect.

If your career record demonstrates any of these – or appears to – be ready to reassure your interviewer or to explain why you believe the apparent drawback won't stand in the way of you doing the job effectively. So if they've spotted a gap in your experience that you can't deny, tell them why you believe you can learn on the job.

INSIDE JOB

Even if you know your interviewer and are applying for an internal post, the interview should still be conducted as if you were an external applicant. For one thing, it means all the candidates can be asked the same questions and therefore be assessed on an equal footing. And for another thing, your interviewer will want to hear how you answer certain questions, even if they already know the facts. So don't feel uncomfortable. Answer questions as you would to a stranger, except that you can add phrases such as, 'As you know …,' or 'You'll remember …' to your answers if this feels easier.

The more time you have, the better you should be able to work out what questions you're likely to be asked. Clearly you will be asked about your relevant skills, qualifications and experience in the key areas of responsibility outlined in the job description.

You are also likely to be asked for your opinions or views on the key responsibilities – questions such as, 'What do you think are the most important techniques for working under pressure?' if the job involves a lot of stress and tight deadlines. Or, if it involves detailed figurework, questions like, 'How do you make sure that you don't make any errors in your figurework?'

On top of these kinds of questions, you can also expect to be asked about anything notable – good or bad – on your CV and application form. So with a bit of time to think about it, you should be able to anticipate the gist of a good proportion of the key questions you're going to be asked.

Be ready to reassure your interviewer or to explain why you believe the apparent drawback won't stand in the way of you doing the job effectively

5 the questions

The core of the interview is of course the questions themselves. So if you're tight for time, this is where you want to focus most of your preparation. We've already seen how you should be able to anticipate many of the questions you're going to be asked. So as you go through this list you should be able to see at a glance which questions you need to be ready with an answer for.

To help you find your way around this chapter, you'll find it divided into questions on different topics:

1. **questions about why you've applied for the job**
2. **questions about you**
3. **questions about your career**
4. **questions for graduates**
5. **questions about your personality**
6. **the nightmare questions.**

Many questions are variations on others, and once you've got the hang of the kinds of answers you need to give, you'll be able to work many of them out for yourself. The questions here are the most typical ones you're likely to be asked.

On top of the questions listed here, you can also expect to be asked specific (and fairly straightforward) questions about your experience, skills, qualifications and anything you've included on your application form or CV.

QUESTIONS ABOUT WHY YOU'VE APPLIED FOR THE JOB

It's not unreasonable for your interviewer to want to know why you're here. And they'll be able to judge how well you'll fit in much better if they

any questions are variations on others, and once you've got the hang of the kinds of answers you need to give, you'll be able to work many of them out for yourself

ththththitthitthinkingsfast

DON'T BE TOO THOROUGH

Although you need to prepare your answers in advance, it's not a good idea to learn them by rote. You'll sound as if you're giving a stilted recitation. In any case, when have you got time to learn every answer by heart? (This is one time when being in a hurry is a plus.) Just prepare the key points you want to make.

know whether you're after job satisfaction or hard cash, career advancement or more convenient working conditions. And what's wrong with your present job? Are you going to up and leave this new job, too, if they give it to you?

Why do you want this job? Try not to waffle about challenges and prospects. Talk in terms of benefits to them, and be specific about the kind of challenge you enjoy. For example, 'I'm a great organiser, and I'm looking for a post which gives me scope to plan and organise,' or 'I get great satisfaction from leading a successful team, and this job seems to call for someone who can set up and run a tight, well-motivated team.'

Why should we hire you? This is really the same question again.

What appeals most about this job? And so is this one.

What do you think you can bring to this job? And this.

How does this job fit into your career plan? It's dangerous to commit yourself too precisely to a career plan. So you might say something like, 'Business changes so rapidly these days, it's hard to plan precisely. But I know I want to get ahead in this industry/marketing/management and I think the opportunities to do that in this company are excellent.'

Why do you want to leave your present job? 'Because I want to broaden my experience and I think I can do that better in a new organisation.'

Why have you been so long with your present employer? The answer to avoid is one that implies you were getting stale and should have moved earlier. Any answer which contradicts this unspoken worry on the interviewer's part is fine. For example, 'I've been there for several years, but in a variety of different roles,' or 'The job was growing constantly, so it felt as though I was undergoing frequent changes without actually changing employer.'

Why have you been such a short time with your present employer? Your interviewer doesn't want to take on someone who is going to leave in six months' time. So show them that you're not really a job-hopper, whatever your CV may appear to show. 'I'd like to settle in one company for several years, but I've found up until now that I've had to move in order to widen my experience and avoid getting stale in the job.'

What do you know about our organisation?
If you respond to this question with a blank stare, you're in trouble. That's why you must know at least something about the organisation. If you're shaky on facts try to muster a few (number of employees, product range or something), and concentrate on ethos: 'I know you're a young, growing organisation with a positive approach to bringing out people's strengths and encouraging them to develop and expand their skills and experience. That's a big part of why I applied for this job.'

thinking smart

MANY QUESTIONS, ONE ANSWER

Be prepared for the interviewer to ask you questions in a different form from those printed here, or prepared in your mind. They may ask you, 'What experience do you have of dealing with difficult customers?' Equally, they may try to elicit the same information by asking, 'Tell me about a difficult customer you've had to deal with. What did you do?' Or even, 'What do you think is the key to dealing with tricky or angry customers?' All of these are essentially different forms of the same question – you will need to be able to recognise them all as being a cue for the answer you've prepared.

QUESTIONS ABOUT YOU

Your interviewer wants to know what kind of person you are, what your style of work is, how you go about tackling a job, what sort of manager you are, and so on. These questions are all designed to elicit this information from you.

Tell me about yourself This is not an invitation to give your life history. You should aim to describe the kind of person you are in a couple of minutes at most. Concentrate on positive qualities, and link them to the key responsibilities of the job you're applying for. For example, 'I'm a people person – I enjoy working with people and being part of a team. I'm the sort of person who likes to get stuck into a project, and I really enjoy seeing a project right through from initial planning to the final stages ...' and so on.

What sort of person are you? This is the same question again.

What motivates you? You need to give an answer, as always, that also benefits your potential employer and links into the key responsibilities of the job. So don't say, 'My pay packet.' Give an answer such as, 'I'm happiest when I can see a project through from start to finish,' or 'I get a real kick out of running a team that is happy and knows it is successful.'

What are your strengths? Go for it. This is a perfect question – just focus your answers on the key responsibilities of the job to make sure your strengths are relevant to your interviewer.

What is your management style? There's no point in lying to questions like this, so give an honest answer. But again, make sure it's relevant. You don't need to give a 20-minute rant on the subject; just a couple of clear sentences will do: 'I prefer a carrot rather than a stick approach, and I have an open-door policy,' or 'I believe a manager has to be firm with the team, and the team appreciate it so long as you are also scrupulously fair.' It helps to follow this with an anecdote – some instance of a problem in the team which you resolved firmly but fairly, for example.

How do you work in a team? The same applies here. Give a brief answer and follow it with an anecdote or example demonstrating what you mean. If teamwork is an important part of the job, you should expect this question (or a variant of it) and have an anecdote ready. The same principle applies to any other questions of the same type, such as:

- ▸ **How do you approach a typical project?**
- ▸ **How do you get the best from people?**
- ▸ **How do you operate under stress?**

What would your colleagues say about you? This is an invitation to list your strong points, so grab it. Concentrate on your plus points as a colleague – supportive, a good team player and so on. As with all these questions, it's unwise to make any outrageous claims. You could well come unstuck if your references are checked out or when you start the job if you're offered it. But of course you'll put the best complexion on things. So if you're a bit of a loner but get on with everyone, you might give an answer like, 'They'd say I was one of the quieter members of the team, popular and can be relied on to pull with the team when it's facing any kind of challenge.'

What would your boss say about you? Your interviewer may well be your prospective boss, so be careful. They want to know that you're an effective worker, but they don't want you stepping on their toes. So describe yourself as any boss would want to see you. For example, 'My boss would describe me as hard working, easy to motivate and

Give a brief answer and follow it with an anecdote or example demonstrating what you mean

loyal. She'd say that I work well on my own initiative, and I'm a supportive member of the team.' Resist the temptation to say 'I *think* my boss would say ...' Be positive and certain in your answer.

QUESTIONS ABOUT YOUR CAREER

Does your profile match the kind of person the interviewer is looking for? Are you at the right point on the career ladder? Where are you planning to go from here? Has your past career progress fitted you for this job? Will you expect promotion and, if so, will you want it at about the same time they'll be ready to promote you?

thinking smart

GIVE ME AN EXAMPLE

Your interviewer is likely to ask you for examples of your experiences. So be ready to give them. For instance, if they want to know what you're like at dealing with crises, they are likely to ask something like, 'Can you give me an example of a crisis you've encountered at work, and tell me how you handled it?' You've already identified the key areas of expertise your interviewer will want you to demonstrate, so prepare examples to illustrate each one.

Where do you see yourself in five years' time?
This is very similar to the earlier question about
how you think this job fits in with your career
plans. You want to be careful because, if you give a
specific goal and the interviewer knows they
cannot fulfil it, they will be put off hiring you. So
keep it open. But remember that they want to
know you have drive and will keep increasing your
value to them. Say something like, 'I'm certainly
ambitious, and I like to keep moving and
progressing. But you can't fit a job to a preset list
of conditions. I find it's far more rewarding to let
the job lead you forward.'

What are your long-term career plans? This is
the same question again under a different guise.

***How long would you expect to stay with this
company?*** The interviewer isn't going to employ
someone who'll be off again before they've got
their full value from them. So indicate that you'd
like to stay a few years. 'I'd like to settle with this
company and grow and develop within in. I see
myself staying as long as I keep progressing here.'

When would you expect promotion? Don't give
a firm timescale here. The answer is, you should
expect promotion when you deserve it. 'I would

Remember that they want to know you have drive and will keep increasing your value to them

hope to be promoted once I have demonstrated my value to the company, and shown that I'm worth it. That's why I want to join a company that is growing so that the promotion opportunities will be there when I'm ready to move up.'

QUESTIONS FOR GRADUATES

Your interviewer is likely to want to know about your university career, and how it has helped to make you suitable for this job. From what subject you read to what your extra-curricular interests were, you can expect to answer questions on these topics if this is your first or second job since graduating.

thfhi**thinking smart**

BITE YOUR LIP

Whatever the temptation, don't argue with your interviewer. If they see you as difficult and argumentative it will put them off employing you. They may even be testing you to see how you respond to their belligerent questioning. So if you tell them you run a team of three people and they say, 'That's hardly managing, is it? This job entails running a team of 10', don't get defensive. Say something like, 'I can see that it looks very different on the surface, but I'd say the same principles apply whether you manage one person or a hundred.'

Why did you choose your particular course? Try to come up with something more interesting than 'I liked the subject.' If it doesn't obviously relate to the job you're applying for, use it to demonstrate some natural skill or ability: 'I've always been good at anything scientific – I have a very analytical mind. And this course seemed to be ideal for honing and extending my natural skills.'

How do you think your studies relate to this job? You'll only be asked this if it isn't obvious. Draw any relevant comparisons you can, but you can also say, 'I think the discipline of learning any subject at university teaches you self-motivation, communication skills and trains your mind to continue learning new skills. And those are all vital to being a success in business.'

What project work have you done? What your interviewer really wants to know is how your project work has helped prepare you for this job. So describe it by way of explaining how it called for great teamwork, or detailed research, or whatever it required that you know is relevant to this job.

What extra-curricular activities did you do? Your extra-curricular exploits say a lot about you. There's a world of difference between the kind of

person who joins the theatrical society as a performer, and one who runs the chess club or organises the student branch of CAMRA. So again, highlight the activities which demonstrate that you have the skills or qualities your interviewer is looking for. You don't have to list every group you belonged to; just pick out the relevant ones.

QUESTIONS ABOUT YOUR PERSONALITY

And what about you? What kind of person will they be employing if they take you on? It's not unreasonable for your interviewer to want to know something about you. After all, they need to assess whether you'll get on with the people you'll be working closest with. And your personal

thinking smart

NO NEED FOR CRITICISM

Don't criticise your current employer, or any previous ones. Find polite ways to indicate real problems if they must be mentioned, but don't sound bitchy or as though you have a chip on your shoulder. *You* may know your complaints are justified, but to your interviewer they may just make you sound like a carping whinger who is likely to talk about them in the same terms if they employ you.

interests can tell them a lot about you in other ways too, such as whether you enjoy solo or group activities, for example.

How would your friends describe you? 'What friends?' is the wrong answer to this question. In fact, it runs along much the same lines as 'How would your colleagues describe you?' Don't be unrealistic about yourself, but pick out the strongest points which will be relevant. It's always worth mentioning loyalty and supportiveness.

What outside interests do you have? Your interviewer is trying to find out more about you. Your interests will tell them whether you are sporty, competitive, enjoy dangerous hobbies, like solo or group activities, and so on. Don't invent hobbies (you don't want your interviewer to say, 'Bungee jumping? Me too! Where's your favourite location round here for a jump? What kind of equipment do you use?'), but select those hobbies or interests that show you as the kind of person your interviewer is looking for.

What have you read and enjoyed lately? Don't make up some fashionable answer here, or name a leading business book you haven't actually read. You may be asked questions about your answer. You

Highlight the activities which demonstrate that you have the skills or qualities your interviewer is looking for

don't really have to mention the *most recent* book you've read, so just pick one you've genuinely enjoyed which is slightly offbeat – you're not one of the crowd. You might want to choose an unusual classic, an avant-garde title or a biography – pick something that will show a side of you you'd like the interviewer to see.

THE ILLEGAL QUESTION

Certain questions are technically illegal, or can be if there isn't a sound, relevant reason for asking them. These include questions relating to your race, religion or sex, questions about your medical history, or about your future plans for a family, that sort of thing. But what do you do if you're asked? You can obviously answer if you wish to, but what if you'd rather not? While you're perfectly entitled to get defensive and demand that your interviewer retract the question, such behaviour may not help you get this job. Your best bet is to say politely, 'Can I ask why you need to know that?' Unless there's a legitimate reason, this will almost certainly lead to a retraction. If they persist in asking you something totally unreasonable, you will have to choose between refusing firmly or answering anyway (whether truthfully or not).

THE NIGHTMARE QUESTIONS

Some interviewers are deliberately testing you. Not to be cruel for the sake of it – they'll be doing it to everyone else too (or at least everyone they think is worth testing). And some questions are just very tough to answer even if the interviewer isn't trying to make it hard for you. It's worth being ready to answer this kind of question; after all, if you're ready for this, you're ready for anything.

What are your weaknesses? There is a whole raft of questions which invite you to say something negative about yourself. Resist. The best defense to use against all these is one of the following:

- ▶ humour ('My greatest weakness is food')

- ▶ something personal, not work related ('I'm useless at getting round to household jobs – changing lightbulbs and fixing leaky taps')

- ▶ something from long ago, which you have now learnt from ('Fifteen years ago I'd have said paperwork, but I've learnt to set aside half an hour at the start of every day for it. Now I reckon I'm more on top of the paperwork than the rest of my colleagues')

- ▶ Something which your interviewer will see as a strength ('I'm dreadful at stopping in the middle of something. I tend to stay at work until a task is done, even though my family often complain that I'm late home').

You don't really have to mention the *most recent* book you've read, so just pick one you've genuinely enjoyed which is slightly offbeat – you're not one of the crowd

What sort of people do you find it difficult to work with? Again, you need to resist criticising other people. Don't be drawn into bitching about the PR in your department who's always trying to boss people around, or the programmer who is always moaning about their workload. Start by saying that you generally find most people are easy to work with, but if you had to pick a type you found difficult it would be people who don't pull their weight, and don't seem to care about the standard of their work.

What do you dislike most at work? You love work, remember? This interviewer can safely hire you, knowing that you will be well motivated every minute of your working life. So if asked, you can't think of anything you dislike. The only possible exception is if this job is very different from your last, in which case you might say something like, 'I really enjoy my work. But occasionally I get a little frustrated in a small company that I don't get to meet customers as often as I'd like. That's one of the reasons why this job appeals to me so much.'

Describe a difficult situation which, with hindsight, you could have handled better. Again, the trick here is to be ready with something from a long time ago. And try to prepare an example where it really wasn't your fault you handled it as you did. For example, 'With hindsight, I can see that it would have been quicker to evacuate everyone straight down the main staircase rather than use the fire escape, but because the phones were down I had no way of knowing that the main staircase was safe.'

What sort of decisions do you find difficult?
You've never found a decision difficult in your life, of course. But the danger with some of these questions is that if you come across as being too implausibly perfect, you risk sounding glib and arrogant. So you have to admit to some minor failings, but make sure they have been overcome or are irrelevant to the job you're applying for – or else make you sound human. So you could say, 'The kind of decisions I dislike most are the ones which other people won't like. They aren't actually difficult, but, for example, I don't like having to make the decision to sack someone.' If you've never had to sack anyone, find another example of something others don't like.

What is your present boss's greatest weakness?
Never criticise any of your past bosses. The

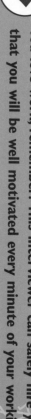

You love work, remember? This interviewer can safely hire you, knowing that you will be well motivated every minute of your working life

interviewer may be your future boss, and wants to hear you being loyal to other bosses even behind their backs. Say something like, 'To be honest, I'm lucky to have a very supportive boss who is good at her job and very easy to work with.' Then look as if you're really trying to think of a weakness. You might add, 'I can't think of anything – if I did it could only be something so picky it wouldn't be worth mentioning.'

Sell me this pen. Some interviewers like asking this kind of question even if you're not applying for a sales post. The aim is to see that you focus not on features ('It's solid silver') but on the benefits to them ('It will impress people'). So give them four or five benefits of the pen (or notepad, or paperclip or whatever they've asked you to sell them), and then finish, half jokingly, with a standard closing technique: 'Shall I put you down for two dozen?' or 'Would you prefer it in black or red?'

Tell me a story. This is a semi-trick question. You're supposed to demonstrate whether you have a sufficiently logical mental approach to ask for the question to be more specific before you answer it. So ask the interviewer, 'What kind of story?' They will probably ask for a story about you, and are likely to specify whether they want a work-related or a personal story. Then just relate some anecdote which shows you in a good light.

What do you think about privatisation/global warming/the Balkans (or whatever)? The interviewer is trying to find out how much of an interest you take in the world in general, and also to get an idea of your values and attitude to life. Whatever the topic, you need to demonstrate in your answer that you can see both sides of an argument, that you don't view things in an over-simplistic way, that you can discuss a subject fluently and that you are capable of making judgements. So don't rant on about your particular views (if you hold strong views) without acknowledging the other side of the debate. You are most likely to be asked these kind of questions by companies to whom they are relevant. Pharmaceutical companies may ask your views on supplying cost-price drugs to the developing world; banks might ask your views on interest rates. So take into account their likely view on the subject.

Are you talking to other organisations as well as us? You want to show your interviewer that you're in demand. It makes you a more attractive prospect,

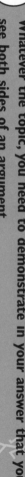

Whatever the topic, you need to demonstrate in your answer that you can see both sides of an argument

and if you're offered the job it can help to push up the salary you manage to negotiate. But at the same time, if you tell them you've had three other offers already, they may be put off you, especially if they still have a long way to go – another round of interviews, for example. So just indicate that you are talking to others and, if it's not a downright lie, you can let them know if you're doing well. For example, 'I've reached the final round of interviews with three other organisations.'

What is your present salary? You don't want to answer this. If you're offered the job, they'll try to get away with paying you as close as they can to your existing salary – at best it will hold the negotiating level down. Say something such as, 'I think salaries can be misleading, as it's really the whole remuneration package that counts. Of course, that's harder to quantify.' Then ask if you can return to the question later, once you get to a point where you need to talk about it in more detail (i.e. when they offer you the job).

What salary are you expecting? You don't want to answer this one either, because there's no chance of getting any more than you say now, and a good chance of scaring them off if you ask too much. So answer a question with a question: 'What salary would you expect to pay for this post?' or ask what salary range has been allocated. If they refuse to answer at this stage, you can reasonably do so too. If they quote a salary and ask for your response, let them know you were thinking of something a little higher, but not out of their reach (assuming you'd agree to that yourself). If they suggest a range, quote them back a range which is higher but overlaps. So if they say £25–28,000 you might say you were thinking of £27–30,000. You're edging them up, but you're not putting them off.

How much do you think you're worth? All these salary questions are good news, essentially. Why would they bother to ask unless they were thinking of offering you the job? This particular question is really the last one again but with a nasty twist to it. It's just a matter of justifying what you're asking for – once you've played the previous game of making them go first. You should already have an idea of the going rate for the job in the industry or the organisation (especially if it's an internal job), so ask for a little more and explain that you've studied salary surveys and so on and, since your experience and skills are above average for the job, you believe you're worth above the average pay. By the way, you can expect the interviewer to respond by saying that the figure you name is too high — that's just part of the negotiating tactic. Don't let it dent your confidence.

The more questions you are ready for, with answers prepared, the more comfortable you will feel going into the interview. So think of as many potential questions as possible, and get a friend or colleague to ask you them so that you can rehearse giving a confident and impressive answer to each one.

If they quote a salary and ask for your response, let them know you were thinking of something a litte higher

6 have you got any questions?

They always ask you this at the end – and quite right too. An interview is a two-way process. Just because they decide they want to offer you the job, it doesn't mean you'll necessarily take it. You might have better offers. So if they have any sense they will want to satisfy all your concerns or questions to persuade you that if they offer you the job, you'll say yes.

You may genuinely have questions you want to ask, which is great. But if you haven't got any, simply saying 'Um … no. No questions, thanks' isn't going to make you look like the dynamic, incisive person you'd like to appear. And what's more, you almost certainly *should* have questions. If you don't ask any, the odds are you'll miss out on information you could have discovered … if only you'd asked.

Of course, you want to ask sensible, intelligent questions. You won't impress your interviewer by asking questions like, 'What colour will my office chair be?' or 'Will my desk be near a window?' Equally, you don't want to come across as work-shy with questions such as, 'How long a lunch break will I get?' or 'How early do most people leave the office on a Friday?'

THE QUESTIONS

So what are you going to ask? Well, you're going to ask questions which make you look intelligent, enthusiastic, commited and ambitious. Questions

thinking smart

SHOW YOU'RE KEEN

It's important to let your interviewer know that you want the job – it could influence their decision on whether to offer it to you. So when they ask, 'Any questions?', reply by saying something like, 'Yes, I have. I would certainly be interested in joining this company, and there are one or two things I'd like to know …' This kind of positive response really does make a difference. If it comes to a choice between you and one other impressive candidate, it can tip the balance in your favour.

about holiday entitlements, working hours, and so on, can wait until you've been offered the job. So here are a few ideas for you.

Why has this vacancy come up? This is a sensible question, and one which may have been covered earlier in the interview. But if it hasn't, you can ask it now. If there happens to be anything fishy going on, you will probably pick up clues from the answer. Most vacancies are entirely reasonable, but some people leave because the job is frustrating or a certain colleague or superior is impossible to work with. If this is the case, you want to know. If you receive a non-commital answer to your question – such as 'The person doing the job at the moment is leaving' – you might want to probe a little deeper.

There are two ways of doing this. One is to ask directly, 'Are they leaving for any reason that I need to know about?' If there is something you should know, it's going to be difficult for the interviewer to avoid telling you. If they do sidestep the question again, that in itself should be a clue to you that things aren't right. If your interviewer is getting defensive and you don't want to appear pushy, you can always let the matter drop for now. If you are offered the job, however, pursue it further at that stage.

The other, less forward approach to gleaning more about why the present incumbent is leaving is simply to ask how long they have been in the job. If they've only been there a few months, it's reasonable to ask why they are moving on so soon. If they have been there for several years, the chances are they were simply ready for a change. However, if you detect any defensiveness in your interviewer you should still make a note to follow up this question if you're offered the job.

Do you promote internally when possible? If you're asking questions about promotion, that shows you're keen to do well and you plan to move up the organisation. As a supplementary question, you can also ask whether the company or the division is expanding at the moment.

What opportunities are there to gain extra qualifications or experience? You want to be careful with questions about training if you've applied for the job setting yourself up as an expert in your field. But if this isn't the case, or if you are a professional such as an accountant or legal specialist who would expect to add to your qualifications, go ahead and ask. Again, it shows you want to improve your career prospects and increase your value to the company.

If you're asking questions about promotion, that shows you're keen to do well and you plan to move up the organisation

DON'T TAKE OVER

Bear in mind that, when you start asking questions, most interviewers will resent it if they feel you are trying to take control and start, in effect, to interview *them*. So remain deferential and make sure you don't inadvertently take over. It helps, for example, to start questions with phrases like, 'May I ask ...?' rather than launching into an interrogative , 'Tell me ...' style of approach.

What will be the top priority in this job over the next six months? This is an extremely useful question to know the answer to, and it also shows that your focus is on the overall objectives of the job, so you're less likely to get bogged down in day-to-day routine and fail to meet your targets. It also has the psychological advantage of projecting into the future and inviting your interviewer to envisage you in the job.

If you have a second interview with someone else, it's well worth asking this question again. It's useful to see if there is a consistent view as to what your key objective should be.

If I were offered this job, where would you see me in five years' time? Again, you're asking your interviewer to imagine you in the job. You're also showing a long-term commitment to the company and indicating that you'd want to progress upwards. The answer is also going to be very informative – how fast do careers move in this organisation, and in what direction? You need this information if you're offered the job.

Do you have any reservations about my ability to do this job? This question can be prefixed with a confident statement along the lines of, 'I'm very interested in this job, and I believe I could do it well …' It may seem like a pushy question but, in fact, it's perfectly reasonable. You're a salesperson, selling yourself as the ideal employee in this post, and you need to know whether your buyer has any outstanding sales objections. Why shouldn't you ask?

If they say they have none, they are saying they have no reason not to offer you the job – a very useful admission to draw from them. If they *do* have reservations they'll have to express them, and you'll get a final chance to reassure them.

Most interviewers will resent it if they feel you are trying to take control and start, in effect, to interview them

When can I expect to hear from you? This may have been covered already, but if not you should ask it. And make it your last question. Apart from the fact that you need to know this, it gives you another potential advantage. If they fail to get in touch by the date they say they will, it gives you a legitimate reason to contact them and chase them up.

Not only does this stop you being on tenterhooks for so long, it can have a practical use, too. What if you're offered another job in the interim? And suppose you have to give them a prompt answer? If you've been promised a response from this interview by a certain date it makes it easier to put gentle pressure on the interviewer to meet that deadline.

These questions should give you plenty of scope for sounding both intelligent and prepared (even if _you_ know you didn't start thinking about this interview until a couple of hours ago). You need ask only a couple of questions to impress your interviewer, although you can ask more if you have more.

If some of these questions sound a little pushy to you, remember that the phrasing makes a big difference. It is certainly possible to ask, 'Do you have any reservations about my ability to do this

DRAWN A BLANK?

What if you really don't have a single question? Your mind's gone blank, or you didn't have time to prepare any questions? You want to sound intelligent, but you just can't think of anything to ask. In that case, say something like, 'I did have plenty of questions, but we've covered them all during our discussions.' If possible, add a clue as to what the questions were about; for example, 'I was particularly interested to know what your future plans for the job were, but we've dealt with that thoroughly.'

job?' in a way which is firm – even a little aggressive. If you're a confident kind of person with a no-nonsense interviewer, this probably won't bother you. But it is equally possible to ask it in a gentle, non-confrontational way. Begin, 'May I ask …', and carry on from there.

If you're at all nervous about any of these questions, practise them (out loud if possible) until you find a way of asking them that you feel comfortable with.

Try to come up with questions you genuinely want to know the answers to – the ones in this chapter are not definitive, they are merely guides and suggestions. Save the practical questions about hours of work and all that stuff until you're offered the job (the interviewer may well tell you this anyway, without you asking). Recognise that asking questions has a dual purpose:

- ▶ to acquire any additional information you need
- ▶ to impress your interviewer with your incisive, intelligent and focused approach.

Prepare your questions in advance and then practise them out loud – with a friend or colleague role-playing the part of the interviewer if possible – until you find a way of asking them that you feel relaxed with.

Try to come up with questions you genuinely want to know the answers to

7 tests

Uh-oh. Scary. Your prospective employer may ask you to take some kind of test to help you assess whether you are suitable for the job. Many of us don't enjoy tests at the best of times, and even those of us who quite enjoy them can get nervous if the outcome is going to influence our chances of getting a job we really want.

There aren't any golden rules for passing tests, and many of them aren't geared towards passing or failing, but towards assessing your personality or abilities. But if you are prepared for the tests, and know what to expect, it doesn't half help. So here's a brief guide to the kind of tests you may be asked to perform.

APTITUDE TESTS

These can require full written answers or they may be multiple-choice questions. All you can really do is answer them as well as possible. They tend to be used to test technical skills so, if you have the necessary skills to do the job, you should walk the test. The only thing to watch out for here is that you read and follow all instructions carefully. Most written tests are exactly what they appear to be, but don't be caught out. Occasionally, tests can include hidden catches such as asking you to read the whole paper before answering any of the questions. If you don't (and frankly, who does unless they've been warned), you'll find as you put your pen down that the fine print at the end tells you not to write down any of your answers.

PSYCHOLOGICAL TESTS

These aptitude tests are intended to assess your personality type. They will tell your prospective employer whether you are, for example, outgoing or introverted, a good team player or someone who works best alone, full of ideas or most effective putting other people's ideas into operation. Psychological tests can involve anything from a multiple-choice questionnaire to a whole day of role-playing or practical exercises.

There's no point in worrying about these tests (I know that's easier said than done). But the good news is that there is no right or wrong in these tests, there aren't better or worse types of personality you could be assessed as. Your prospective employer is looking for someone who will fit in with the rest of the team. If there's already a terrific ideas person, for instance, they may not

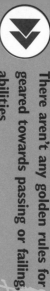

There aren't any golden rules for passing tests, and many of them aren't geared towards passing or failing, but towards assessing your personality or abilities

want another one. Or perhaps what they really need is someone who can follow a project through and take care of the details. The fact is, you've no idea what your prospective employer is looking for, so you might as well answer honestly.

TEAM TESTS

You may be asked to take part in exercises as part of a team, possibly with other candidates or perhaps with existing employees. This kind of test generally lasts all day or even over a couple of days. It might involve anything from hiking across the moors to building a model of the Eiffel Tower out of paperclips. You will be observed and assessed throughout the test.

One positive point to bear in mind here is that these tests are expensive to run, and your

thinking smart

TEST VIRGIN?

Let the tester know if you've never taken a psychometric test. Some of them get easier if you've done them before – your tester will know if this applies to the one they're asking you to do. If so, make sure they're aware that you don't have that advantage.

prospective employer wouldn't be spending their money unless they felt the job warranted it and you were worth the investment. So simply being asked to take part in the test is a confidence boost.

Unless you're applying for a job as a park ranger, it's unlikely your prospective employer gives two hoots whether you can hike across the moors. It is also unlikely that they really need a model of the Eiffel Tower in paperclips. No, what they want to know is how you function in a team. You can't spend the time trying to be someone you're not – and if you got the job on that basis you wouldn't be happy in it anyway. You are likely to be put under sufficient pressure that you'll have a hard time putting on a complete act for the duration in any case.

So be aware that it's your team performance that counts, not the project you've been set. Be yourself but avoid the extremes which may deter the assessors from recommending you:

▸ **Don't take over officiously and become too bossy (although if the team genuinely defers to you as its leader that's fine).**

▸ **Don't be so quiet and reserved that you seem uninvolved. Make sure you make enough of a contribution to be assessed on.**

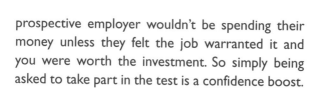

Unless you're applying for a job as a park ranger, it's unlikely your prospective employer gives two hoots whether you can hike across the moors

- Don't argue with other team members. If conflict arises, play the diplomat and be seen to be trying to improve matters.

- Don't opt out and refuse to play the game, saying 'This is stupid! What's the point of building an Eiffel Tower anyway?'

- If there are other teams competing with yours, it's a good thing to show a competitive streak, but not to the point of ruthlessness. Adopt the approach that, 'It's only a game, but all things being equal we'd prefer to win it and we'll give it our best shot.' You are not more likely to get the job because your team was first to complete its paperclip construction. It's how you play the game that counts.

Apart from being the diplomat, the most useful roles you can take on in the team, to impress you assessors, are:

- Keep the team focused on the objective: 'Hey, guys, does it really matter how we string the paperclips together? Let's concentrate on getting the tower built – we can each string them together in our own way.'

- Summarise how the team is doing from time to time: 'So we've worked out how to construct the thing, and we've decided not to try and incorporate a working elevator. That means we need to think about allocating tasks next.'

All tests are, essentially, just another way of finding out about you, the same as the interview itself. The aim is not to torture you, trick you or put you through the hoop, but simply to establish whether you are the best candidate for the job. So your best approach is to take the tests in your stride, be yourself and answer questions honestly.

for next time

If you are going to be given a long or complex test, your prospective employer will forewarn you. If this happens ask if the test is a standard one and, if so, which test it is. You'll find there are several books on the market which explain most of the popular tests and tell you what to expect. Even if you don't know which test you'll be doing, you can read through descriptions of most of the likely ones and you'll be well prepared. After all, all your fellow candidates are in the same boat, and probably at least as nervous as you.

All tests are, essentially, just another way of finding out about you, the same as the interview itself

8 controlling your nerves

No, I can't tell you how to make your nerves go away completely. Sorry. But it is possible to keep them sufficiently under control so they don't interfere with your performance at interview. When something is really important to us, it's only natural that we should get nervous about it. Some of us manage to feel confident regardless, and to project that confidence to the interviewer. Others of us shake, blush, stammer and go rigid.

Unless you are applying for a job where nerves are a no-no – for example, where you'll be expected to run frequent presentations to large numbers of important customers – your interviewer will almost certainly sympathise with you and want to put you at your ease. So long as your nerves don't get in the way of the interview, they won't mark you down for being a bit shaky.

But what can you do to minimise the effect of your nervousness? Well, you can:

- ▶ Take preventive action.
- ▶ Relax.
- ▶ Rehearse.

PREVENTIVE ACTION

One of the simplest measures you can take to ease the nerves is to avoid any obvious sources of stress. For example:

- ▶ Make sure you wear clothes that are easy and comfortable. You don't want to be worrying about buttons coming undone, or find that once you've sat down your clothes have got you in a half-Nelson.

- ▶ If you are worried about fumbling over your briefcase or bag, or spilling your papers across the floor, take a single envelope file in with you. If you drop it, it will stay in one piece. You can always leave the rest of your stuff at reception.

- ▶ If you are at all worried you will be shaky, politely turn down any offers of coffee or tea. If you worry that your mouth will go dry, you can always ask for a glass of water – you don't have to drink it (or indeed touch it) if you think the danger of spilling it is greater than the risk of your mouth turning into a desert. But you've got it there if you need it.

Some of us manage to feel confident regardless, and to project that confidence to the interviewer. Others of us shake, blush, stammer and go rigid

You may have other worries – in that case look for ways you can sidestep the risk and avoid the issue altogether.

RELAX

You haven't got time for embarking on a six-month course of yoga to bring your overall stress levels down, or meditating for half an hour every morning or evening. Such techniques work very well over the long term for some people, but they won't do you much good right now.

What you need are last-minute stress busters to keep the nerves at bay. So here are some suggestions that should help:

- Don't try to do an interview on an empty stomach. Make sure you have a light breakfast or lunch.

- Don't drink before an interview, however tempting a stiff drink may be before an afternoon interview.

- Relax your body by breathing in and out slowly. Breathe in through your nose, and out through your mouth. Get your rib cage to expand and your diaphragm to push down as you breathe. Before the interview, do this with your eyes shut if possible. But in the interview just a single slow breath in and out while the interviewer is speaking should be a big help, and will be imperceptible to them.

> **FINAL CHECK**
> Five minutes before your interview, nip into the cloakroom and quickly check yourself in the mirror – teeth, hair, tie, earrings, buttons, zips. That way you won't need to worry about such details when you get into the interview.

REHEARSE

The real cure for nerves is confidence. So to dispel the worst of your nerves and reduce them to a level where they simply keep you on your toes, you need to be confident. And the best way to achieve confidence is to rehearse until you're sure of what you're doing.

Now, I know we're tight for time here, but at least you can rehearse your opening greeting. Most of us find the nerves are worst at the start and then reduce gradually as we realise we're not making a complete prat of ourselves after all. So practise holding out your hand for a firm handshake and saying, 'Good morning. Pleased to meet you,' or whatever you want to say. Practise in front of a mirror, and then get a friend to take the role of interviewer.

One of the simplest measures you can take to ease the nerves is to avoid any obvious sources of stress

If you have time between now and the interview, you can adopt the same approach with any questions that you are partciularly worried about answering and which you think you are likely to be asked. When they come up, you'll find yourself sighing with relief rather than sweating with worry.

for next time

Practice and rehearsal really are the key to controlling nerves. So when you have time (and you'll be leaving much more time next time, won't you?) spend as much of it as you need to running through your interview, answering likely questions and so on until you feel confident that you know what you're doing. Enlist other people to help you, taking the role of interviewer.

Most of us find the nerves are worst at the start and then reduce gradually as we realise we're not making a complete prat of ourselves after all

9 the follow-up

The interview's over and you can breathe a sigh of relief. Well, yes you can, but it's not all over yet. There's still useful work to be done while you're waiting to hear from your prospective employer. And even once you've heard, there's still action you can take.

WHILE YOU'RE WAITING

There are two things to do after the interview and before you hear whether you have been successful. The first thing to do is to write a thank-you letter to your interviewer. In fact, since we're thinking fast here, why not e-mail it? That way you'll be sure of getting in there before they make their decision.

Your thank-you letter has two purposes:

1. It enables you to remind the interviewer who you are, in the same way an advertisement does.

2. It gives you a chance to mention (*briefly*) anything important you missed saying at the interview itself.

Since you will almost certainly be the only candidate who writes following the interview, it will do a lot to bring your name to the interviewer's attention, even if you had slipped down the list. It can make the difference, for example, between whether or not you get on to the shortlist for final interview. It shows you are keen on the job, commited and courteous with it.

So what's the letter going to say? It should say something along the lines of: *Thank you for seeing me this morning. I very much enjoyed meeting you and I would like to confirm that I am still very interested in the post. I look forward to hearing from you.*

You may also want to add a brief note along the lines of: *By the way, we discussed the possibility of working overseas, and I forgot to mention that I have previously taken evening language courses in both French and Spanish.* There's no need to add this kind of information unless there's something important you feel you omitted, and a single sentence will do fine. This is no place to launch into a long, defensive ramble because you think the interviewer had some reservation about your suitability and you feel like repeating what you've already said at the interview.

Now, there's one more thing you'll need to do while you're waiting to hear: make notes about the interview. Any general points you note about how it went will help with other interviews – do you feel you were well prepared, were you confident enough, did you ramble too much, were you too flippant, did you answer questions fluently? These are useful points to note for yourself so you can handle your next interview even better.

There's another reason, too, for making notes. You may get a second interview. In that case you need to note:

- the names of your interviewer(s) and anyone else you met

- any questions you feel you could have dealt with better (so you can prepare more next time)

- any reservations you suspect the interviewer may have been left with

- anything you wish you had said but didn't

- anything which seemed to impress them and will therefore be worth reinforcing next time.

IF YOU ARE OFFERED THE JOB

Congratulations. If you want the job and are offered it, accept it happily – subject to negotiations if important areas of pay and conditions haven't been dealt with already. If you know you don't want it – you hated the company or you've got a better offer – that's fine too. Turn the job down, but do it politely. You never know when you might encounter people again, and it won't help if you once told them, however honestly, that they could stick their job and you wouldn't work for them if they paid you a million pounds.

The problem comes, however, when you're offered a job while you're still waiting to find out if you're going to get a better offer from someone else. You don't want to say yes and then miss out on the better job. But you don't want to say no if you might *not* be offered the other job. Hmmm.

Your first response in this situation should be to play for time. Say you're delighted to be offered the job and please can you get back to them in, say, 24 hours. It's not going to be reasonable to leave it too long, and they'll guess what's going on if you ask for

thinking smart

PIG IN THE MIDDLE

Technically, your new job isn't guaranteed until you have been offered it in writing, with a contract stipulating pay and conditions, and you have returned a written acceptance. So don't hand in your notice until this process is complete, otherwise you could end up with no job at all.

It won't help if you once told them, however honestly, that they could stick their job and you wouldn't work for them if they paid you a million pounds

several days to decide. No one wants to be second best, so don't let them know you're hoping for a better offer. If they ask why you need time to decide, you can say that you want to talk it over with your family. Or simply say that taking on a new job is a big decision and you don't like to rush big decisions. They can't argue with that.

It's perfectly reasonable to get in touch with your preferred employer at this stage and explain the problem. They'll be pleased to be your first choice, and if they think everyone else wants to employ you too, that makes you look like an even better prospect. Don't expect an instant answer from them, but ask them if they could get back to you by tomorrow. They can always say no.

If this sounds like a good technique for getting an offer out of your first choice employer even if you haven't really been offered another job, it isn't. Don't go there. If they were going to offer you the job anyway it may well persuade them to offer fast before they lose you. And it may work if they were tossing up between you and one other candidate. But if you were a borderline choice it is as likely to bounce them into saying no to you if they don't want the time pressure. But at least a firm no now leaves you free to accept the other offer, rather than wonder whether to turn it down and then risk ending up with nothing.

It may be that your first choice employer is nowhere near making a decision. Perhaps you haven't even been interviewed yet, or maybe they're still drawing up a shortlist for second interviews. Or maybe your first choice is internal promotion and you're reluctant to tell your boss that you've been applying for jobs elsewhere. In this case, I'm afraid there is nothing you can do but gamble. You'll have to weigh up how much you want this new job, how much you'd mind staying in the job you're in now, your chances of getting the job you *really* want, and so on. But remember – you're obviously employable and you can give a good interview (even when you've left it so late). The fact that this interviewer has offered you the job is a very good sign.

IF YOU DON'T GET THE JOB

If you miss out on a job you were really keen to get, that's no reason to give up on it entirely. The person they offer the job to instead may in the end take up a better offer. Or they may accept the job but it may not work out for them and they might leave within a few months. Even if they are

It's perfectly reasonable to get in touch with your preferred employer at this stage and explain the problem. They'll be pleased to be your first choice

successful in the job, a close colleague may leave before too long.

You want to make sure that if any of these is the case, your name is the next one on the list. So send a polite reply to your letter of rejection, showing that you're still in the job market. Resist any temptation to suggest that you'd have been a better choice, or that the person they've appointed will turn out to be a mistake. Question your interviewer's judgement and you might as well not bother to write at all.

Say something along the lines of: *Thank you for letting me know the outcome of my application, and I'm*

thinking smart

MODEL EMPLOYEE

If the job you miss out on is an internal one, that's a particularly tough thing to cope with. But how you cope may make a big difference to your chances of promotion next time. So no sour grapes, but be genuinely magnanimous and supportive towards the person who lands the job (even if you hate their guts).

sorry I was unsuccessful on this occasion. However, I was very impressed by your company and would still be interested in working for you. I'd be delighted if you would come back to me if things change, or if any other suitable posts arise in the near future.

Your interviewer can't fail to be impressed by your politeness and your commitment and loyalty to their company, and will almost certainly want to call you if another job comes up.

for next time

If you got the job, well done. The next time is likely to be a long way away. But if you didn't, you can start working on your next interview now ... even if you don't yet know what it is. You've made notes of your weak and strong points; now plan responses and start rehearsing and practising ready for next time. You may not have landed this particular job, but keep improving your performance and it's only a matter of time.

If you miss out on a job you were really keen to get, that's no reason to give up on it entirely

your own interview in 15 minutes

Well, this is hardly textbook planning, is it? I've no idea how you got into this position, but you're going to have to think fast to get yourself out of it. My guess is that you wouldn't have let this interview slip so far down your priority list unless you're fairly confident about bluffing your way through – let's hope so anyway. So the best way for you to spend your next 15 minutes is to focus clearly on how you're going to get this job.

Begin by reading Chapter 1, which will tell you what your objective is. No, objectives aren't a waste of time. It won't take long, and it will help you to focus clearly on what you've got to do in the next quarter of an hour.

You should get away with it this time, and if you're the best candidate it ought to show through and you'll win the job

You should get away with it this time, and if you're the best candidate it ought to show through and you'll win the job (whether you deserve it after only 15 minutes' preparation is a matter for your own conscience). I know the work piles up and preparing for an interview gets left to the last minute, but before you go for your next interview (a few days before, that is) have a look at the 'fast thinking gambles' section at the front of this book. It will remind you why you'd be better off starting to prepare earlier for any interview that really matters to you.

But for now, follow the crash course here and you should pull through without giving away your lack of preparation. Thinking fast and acting smart will pay off. Good luck!

1. Now read the job description for the post you're applying for. (You did make sure they sent you a job description, didn't you?) In particular, check out the key responsibilities of the job.

2. For each key responsibility, think of something relevant you can tell the interviewer to show that you have the experience, skill or personal qualities necessary to carry out that responsibility.

3. Put yourself in the interviewer's shoes for a moment. If they have any reservations about your application – long gap between jobs here, lack of experience there, or whatever – what will they be? Once you've identified the key weak spots in your application, come up with a response which will reassure the interviewer.

4. Skip Chapter 3 – it's too late to dither about what to wear, and the adrenaline alone should ensure you come across with sufficient energy and verve.

5. Skim Chapter 4 for a quick guide to what to expect (but if you're starting to panic about the time the next two points are more important).

6. If there are any questions you're worried about how to answer, look through Chapter 5 for a quick guide.

7. Come up with at least one intelligent question to ask your interviewer at the end. Chapter 6 will help.

8. Forget the rest of the book for now; you've run out of time. But read Chapter 9 when you come out of the interview, to find out what to do while you're waiting to hear whether you've got the job.

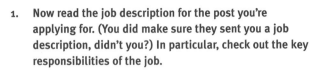

You wouldn't have let this interview slip so far down your priority list unless you're fairly confident about bluffing your way through – let's hope so anyway